Showers Of• Blessings

RAINS OF THE SPIRIT

David O. Oyedepo

CONTENTS

Introduction

And I will make with them a covenant of peace, and will cause the evil beasts to cease out of the land: and they shall dwell safely in the wilderness, and sleep in the woods.

And I will make them and the places round about my hill a blessing; and I will cause the shower to come down in his season; there shall be showers of blessing.

And the tree of the field shall yield her fruit, and the earth shall yield her increase, and they shall be safe in their land, and shall know that I am the Lord, when I have broken the bands of their yoke, and delivered them out of the hand of those that served themselves of them.

Ezekiel 34:25-27

There is a burning desire in my heart, to see the drought in the lives of many Christians come to an end. We have sang the hymn, *"There shall be showers of blessings,"* yet many have never seen dew come down upon them. What they have is at best "mercy drops!"

When we started a series of teachings on the mysteries of God's rainfall in our church, we saw many prophetic utterances come to pass. The dryness in the lives of many, came to an end and their lives became like a watered garden. The dryness in your life will end too, as you read this book, and God will cause you to flourish like a palm tree and grow up like the cedar in Lebanon!

Let me begin by saying that there are four kinds of rain. The rain of righteousness, the rain of the Spirit, the rain of the Word and the rain of blessings. When you talk about rain, what readily comes to the mind of many is the rain of the Spirit and the rain of blessings. But it is a combination of all four types of rain that culminates in what we call, the showers of blessings.

Why is God releasing the showers of blessings upon us? Because by prophecy, the end-time Church is to enjoy a climax of honour and glory as the arrival of the Bridegroom approaches.

In the natural, when a young lady is preparing for her wedding, the honour begins to mount until the climax when she is joined to her spouse.

When it is six months away, you may not know that the wedding is approaching. But when it is about three months to the time, the environment begins to change. Favours begin to pour in from every side. All manner of blessings begin to come. She begins to receive shoes, clothes, trinkets, etc. What began as droplets increases in tempo, until there is a deluge of blessings.

That is what I'am talking about. Our Bridegroom is on His way. He is very close by and the nearer we are to His coming, the more glory we begin to experience.

God has programmed the last days' Church for honour and glory, the kind eyes have not seen nor ears heard. It will be a very unique visitation for you, that is why you must pray for God to grant you divine access to the things I will be teaching in this book. May the Lord grant you understanding.

The Church has entered into its "rainy" season and just like the rainy season is the most glorious season in the natural (where grass is green, leaves on trees are green and fruits can be seen hanging down branches and everything is flourishing), so it is in the realm of the spiritual. Showers cause God's people to flourish (Ps. 65:9-10).

Now, God has decided to rain upon us. He has committed Himself to send us showers of blessings. We must discover what it takes to enjoy the showers to the full.

Please realise that it is the release of the showers from heaven that will make you a man to be envied. Whatever has made men pity you will end, as God rains upon you.

Chapter 1

YOUR ACCESS TO THE RAINS

For I will pour out water upon him that is thirsty, and floods upon the dry ground: I will pour my Spirit upon thy seed, and my blessing upon thine offspring.

Isaiah 44:3

God's will for you is that the dry places of your life become as a well watered garden. He wants to see you "fat" and flourishing, to demonstrate His goodness in practical terms. But it will take His rainfall to accomplish that.

God's rainfall is for the thirsty. It is a basic requirement for enjoying all four kinds of rain in the kingdom of God. Without that genuine thirst, you may never encounter the showers.

Consider the first type of rain, the rain of righteousness. Matthew 5:6 highlights what triggers it off:

> *Blessed are they which do hunger and thirst after righteousness: for they shall be filled.*

So, what do you do to enjoy the rain of righteousness? You hunger and thirst for it! You cannot receive the rain of righteousness without a genuine thirst.

Are you truly desirous? You must first yearn for the outpouring of the rain of righteousness. David yearned for it. He longed to see the rain of righteousness flow. Perhaps he was in a place dry of holiness, dry of God's glory and honour. So he longed for an outpouring of the rain of righteousness.

> *O God, thou art my God; early will I seek thee: my soul thirsteth for thee, my flesh longeth for thee in a dry and thirsty land, where no water is;*
>
> *To see thy power and thy glory, so as I have seen in the sanctuary.*
>
> Psalm 63:1-2

If there is no thirst, there is no access. It takes your yearning desperately for the release of the rain of purity to encounter a deluge. Your strong desire is what leads to its accomplishment.

Then there is the rain of the Spirit, It will also take a thirst, a crave, a yearning to release it.

God wants to pour out upon all flesh the rain of His Spirit, but what may constrain Him from releasing Him to you, is the state of your heart.

He will check to see if you are genuinely thirsty or whether you are asking out of a religious sense—because everyone else is asking!

> *In the last day, that great day of the feast, Jesus stood and cried, saying, If any man thirst, let him come unto me, and drink.*
>
> *He that believeth on me, as the scripture hath said, out of his belly shall flow rivers of living water.*
>
> *(But this spake he of the Spirit, which they that believe on Him should receive: for the Holy Ghost was not yet given; because that Jesus was not yet glorified.)*
>
> John 7:37-39

Basically therefore, a thirst is what you need to release the rain of the Spirit.

The third type of rain is the rain of the Word. You also need a genuine thirst emanating from your heart to contact it.

> *Ho, every one that thirsteth, come ye to the waters,*

*and he that hath no money; come ye, buy, and eat;
yea, come buy wine and milk without money and
without price.*

*Wherefore do ye spend money for that which is not
bread? and your labour for that which satisfieth not?
hearken diligently unto me, and eat ye that which is
good, and let your soul delight itself in fatness.*

Isaiah 55:1-2

The Word of God is likened to water in Ephesians
5:26. It is also described as milk in I Peter 2:2, and strong
meat in Hebrews 5:12-14. The Word is *"that which
satisfieth,"* but you must constantly thirst for it, to be
satisfied by it.

Later in verse eleven of the same Isaiah 55, it is written,
"So shall my word be..."

Therefore, the entire chapter is a prophetic parable on
how to encounter the rain of the Word of God. The
trigger for the rain of revelation or the rain of the Word
is a genuine thirst.

The rain of blessings, which is the fourth type of rain,
answers also to a thirst. Not a thirst for blessings, but
for God!

*But seek ye first the kingdom of God, and his
righteousness; and all these things shall be added
unto you.*

Matthew 6:33

Your delight in God, your thirst for Him, releases the rain of plenty upon you. As long as it is God you are pursuing after, you will not lack any good thing (Ps. 34:10).

It is your thirst for God that opens you up to the rain of His goodies! Job said:

Acquaint now thyself with him, and be at peace: thereby good shall come unto thee.

Job 22:21

David was one of the most prosperous men in the Old Testament. A closer look reveals his dedication to God as the secret behind his rise.

He loved God. His heart panted after God, as a thirsty hart pants after the water brooks (Ps. 42:1). He was not thirsty for goods. No! He was thirsty for God, so good came his way.

In Psalm 122 :1, David declared that he was glad to go into the house of the Lord. In verses 6 - 9, he lets us into his secret winning card:

Pray for the peace of Jerusalem: they shall prosper that love thee.

Peace be within thy walls, and prosperity within thy palaces.

For my brethren and companions' sakes, I will now

13

say, Peace be within thee.

Because of the house of the Lord our God I will seek thy good.

This speaks of commitment, dedication, devotion and addiction to God. It was at the foundation, at the base of his prosperity. This was what established David as a prosperous man.

Many, particularly in the charismatic circle, have left off seeking God and are seeking goods. That is why goods never come to them. David sought the Lord, so he never lacked any good thing (Ps. 34:10).

When Jesus arrived in the New Testament, He incorporated the same principle into the new covenant.

Wherefore, if God so clothe the grass of the field, which to day is, and tomorrow is cast into the oven, shall he not much more clothe you, O ye of little faith?

Therefore take no thought, saying, What shall we eat? or, What shall we drink? or, Wherewithal shall we be clothed?

(For after all these things do the Gentiles seek:) for your heavenly Father knoweth that ye have need of all these things.

But seek ye first the kingdom of God, and his righteousness; and all these things shall be added unto you.

Matthew 6:30-33

God knows you have need of good things, but to encounter His unlimited rain of blessings, you must seek first the kingdom of God and His righteousness. Once you seek the kingdom of God, God then releases the showers of blessings upon you.

In September 1976, I entered into a covenant of total consecration to the Lord. I told the Lord then, "You are either Lord of all or not Lord at all." So, I turned my back on everything else, to face Him. Over twenty years have come and gone and I have not known lack!

Until your Christianity enters the realm of dedication, you cannot be free from frustrations! Just get connected to God by a genuine thirst and not even the devil can stop the flow of blessings to you.

When you become addicted to kingdom pursuits, divine additions become your portion!

It works! I have said countless times, in secret and public places, that I have never prayed for money. Yet, I don't lack an abundance of it! I have found what to seek for that brings blessings in automatically. I hunger and thirst after God, so He guarantees that I never lack the good things of life.

ASKING FOR THE RAIN

Ask ye of the Lord rain in the time of the latter rain;
so the Lord shall make bright clouds, and give them
showers of rain, to every one grass in the field.

Zechariah 10:1

It is not enough to be thirsty for the rains of God, you need to ask for an outpouring upon you. It is he that asks that receives, and he that seeks that finds. You are a grass in the field, so you are entitled to a release of the showers. But you must ask for the rain, in order to get it.

For instance, in Acts 4, the disciples prayed and the place where they were praying shook. They prayed down the rain of the Spirit. You must pray down the rains of God.

Understand that God is eager to give showers of rain to everyone grass in the field. But you must be thirsty for the down pour and express your thirst with a genuine call in prayer.

You have access to the rains of God. Why don't you open up right now with a genuine thirst and ask for the showers?

Chapter 2

THE RAIN OF RIGHTEOUSNESS

Sow to yourselves in righteousness, reap in mercy;
break up your fallow ground: for it is time to seek the
Lord, till he come and rain righteousness upon you.

Hosea 10:12

The greatness of the end-time Church foretold in scriptures, is impossible without the rain of righteousness. It is the fundamental rain of God. It preceeds the release of every other rain and ultimately leads to the glory of the Church.

For instance, we understand that it is impossible to encounter the rain of the Spirit until the rain of righteousness is in place. Acts 2:38 says:

Then Peter said unto them, Repent, and be baptized every one of you in the name of Jesus Christ for the remission of sins, and ye shall receive the gift of the Holy Ghost.

So, the rain of the Spirit follows after repentance, it is sequel to the rain of righteousness.

Look at Jesus Christ. Righteousness was what triggered off the flow of the anointing of the Holy Ghost upon Him (Ps. 45:7). Jesus loved righteousness above all His fellows, so He was anointed with the oil of gladness above them all. He enjoyed unction without measure, because He was pure beyond measure!

The rain of righteousness is also crucial to the release of the rain of the Word. The Bible says:

Seek ye the Lord while he may be found, call ye upon him while he is near:

Let the wicked forsake his way, and the unrighteous man his thoughts: and let him return unto the Lord, and he will have mercy upon him; and to our God, for he will abundantly pardon.

For as the rain cometh down, and the snow from heaven, and returneth not thither, but watereth the earth, and maketh it bring forth and bud, that it may give seed to the sower, and bread to the eater.

Isaiah 55:6-7,10

In essence, God's Word will come on you as the rain

when you forsake every act of wickedness and embrace righteousness.

In Hebrews 9, we discover that the mysteries of life are deposited in the Most Holy place — talking about the tabernacle of Moses and its present day significance. That was where the golden pot that had manna was. That is where the deep things (the profound revelations) are located.

But from verse 7 we come to understand that no unrighteous man ever gains access to these mysteries. Only those sanctified by the blood and yielded to God can proceed into the most holy place.

> *But into the second went the high priest alone once every year, not without blood, which he offered for himself, and for the errors of the people.*
>
> Hebrews 9:7

So, it takes righteousness to enter where the tables of the covenant are just as it takes the rain of consecration to release the rain of revelation.

Until you embrace consecration, you have no access to revelations.

> *And he said unto them, Unto you it is given to know the mystery of the kingdom of God: but unto them that are without, all these things are done in parables:*
>
> *That seeing they may see, and not perceive; and*

hearing they may hear, and not understand; lest at any time they should be converted, and their sins should be forgiven them.

Mark 4:11-12

Reading this, you may wonder, "Who are those without?" Revelation 22:15 says, *"Without are dogs."* Then 2 Peter 2:22 tells us that dogs are those who return to their vomit. These are habitual sinning Christians. They are those who return to the habits they had earlier given up.

Such Christians will never have access to depths of mysteries that make stars of men! Remember, Paul said: *"...the letter killeth, but the spirit giveth life"* (2 Cor. 3:6).

Sinning Christians only have the letter of the Word, lacking the Spirit that will make it produce life. So, it takes the rain of righteousness to experience the rain of revelation.

In the early Church, there was such a strong wave of consecration. The rain of righteousness had been falling, sweeping off dubious characters like Ananias and Sapphira. And because the rain of righteousness was in place, it paved the way for showers of revelation.

And the word of God increased; and the number of the disciples multiplied in Jerusalem greatly; and a great company of the priests were obedient to the faith.

Acts 6:7

If you want to see an increase in revelation in your life, then you must seek for righteousness.

Remember, *"without are dogs"*. How much understanding can you put into a dog? No matter how long he has been your pet, he will never think like a man, he can never become a son.

Clean up! You are a redeemed son of God, to live like a dog is an abuse on your redemption. The lies and immoral acts you are indulging in reduce you to the status of a dog! May God, find you worthy of the rain of the Word.

> **The secret of the Lord is with them that fear him; and he will shew them his covenant.**

Psalm 25:14

The fourth type of rain is the rain of blessing.

Every blessing of God is rooted in righteousness.

> **Who shall ascend into the hill of the Lord? or who shall stand in his holy place?**
>
> **He that hath clean hands, and a pure heart; who hath not lifted up his soul unto vanity, nor sworn deceitfully.**

He shall receive the blessing from the Lord, and righteousness from the God of his salvation.

Psalm 24:3-5

What will this righteous man receive? *"The blessing from the Lord."* Psalm 112:1 also tells us that the man that fears the Lord and delights greatly in His command-ments is blessed. Wealth and riches reside in his house and his seeds become mighty on the earth.

People may mock you for choosing to follow the path of righteousness today. But until men mock you, God cannot make you.

A young lady in our church, caught the Word of righteousness and triumphed by it. In her testimony, she said the electric power corporation disconnected the power supply at the house where she lives because the tenants had connected it illegally. But her co-tenants reconnected the lines.

When she got wind of this, she decided to remain in darkness rather than switch on the illegal power supply. So, she slept in darkness while the others rejoiced in their illegal electricity supply.

This lady became an object of mockery. But God was not asleep He would turn her mourning to dancing. She had also been an applicant, looking for a job. And her present accommodation was a one-room apartment, with shared toilet facilities.

Then mysteriously she got a job with living quarters attached to the package! She also discovered that there was a standby generator attached!

In her testimony, she said, "I have never suffered five minutes *black out* since I left them (her fellow tenants)." God picked her up from their midst. Righteousness exalted her. God was on hand to show Himself strong on her behalf! Halleluyah!

When you embrace righteousness, your journey through life ends up in blessings, no matter what it may look like now. Your beginning may be small, but your latter end shall greatly increase (Job 8:7).

SIN WITHHOLDS THE SHOWERS

And I will lay it waste: it shall not be pruned, nor digged; but there shall come up briers and thorns: I will also command the clouds that they rain no rain upon it.

For the vineyard of the Lord of hosts is the house of Israel, and the men of Judah his pleasant plant: and he looked for judgment, but behold oppression; for righteousness, but behold a cry.

Isaiah 5: 6-7

Why did God command the clouds to rain no more

upon the house of Israel? Because sin reigned in their midst. He looked for judgment, but rather He found oppression and unrighteousness.

Israel was planted on a most fruitful hill. She was the choicest of vines, with a most enviable destiny. But sin withheld her showers from falling.

As I said earlier, we have sang the hymn *"There shall be showers of blessings"*, yet many have never seen any dew come upon them. Even mercy drops are not visible anywhere around them. Because, rather than walking in purity, they prefer to "bombard" heaven with cries!

> *...he looked for judgment, but behold oppression: for righteousness, but behold a cry.*

Stop shutting your heavens! You need the showers! The world is a desert place, you require the showers to make a difference!

Once the sin question is solved, the heavens are opened and the clouds are obliged to release showers upon you.

> *Therefore the showers have been withholden, and there hath been no latter rain; and thou hadst a whore's forehead, thou refusedst to be ashamed.*
>
> Jeremiah 3:3

The devil cannot stop your showers. It is sin that is locking up the heavens above you. As long as sin is present, the rain will be witheld.

So, stop blaming the devil; he is not at fault! I am yet to see any man who is on key with God being stopped by the devil. If he could not stop you giving your life to Christ, then he couldn't possibly be your problem!

It is sin that has locked up your heavens. And whosoever does not refuse sin very soon becomes a piece of refuse!

Righteousness is the choice of the wise. If you choose to, you can purify yourself, even as God is pure (I John 3:3). Using the covenant insights available to you, once you say "No!" to defilement, no devil in hell can defile you.

Who could stop the prodigal son when he arose to go back home? He must have said in his heart, "Enough is enough, I'am going home!" And it was so.

This is the time for our blossoming and flourishing. To refuse to purge yourself is to sign in for shame. When you see others in Zion radiating the glory of God, may shame not chase you out of Zion, and back to Egypt!

Not everyone survives a revival. People whose hearts are not in perfect tune with God, will be swept away by the mighty waves. You will be kept, because you will clean up!

RIGHTEOUSNESS
GUARANTEES FLOURISHING

The righteous shall flourish like the palm tree: he shall grow like a cedar in Lebanon.

Those that be planted in the house of the Lord shall flourish in the courts of our God.

They shall still bring forth fruit in old age; they shall be fat and flourishing.

Psalm 92:12-14

What causes the righteous to flourish are the showers coming from an opened heaven!

When heaven tore open and the Holy Ghost came down upon Jesus, He began to flourish and His fame went abroad. He flourished like the palm tree and like the cedar in Lebanon. He brought forth fruits until the last minute — even on the cross, He saved the sinner crucified beside Him.

The showers of heaven are responsible for the flourishing of the righteous. It is the showers, not his strength or his smartness, or his ability.

God also sends the rain to water seeds in the ground and cause them to yield fruit. Luke 8:11 says:

Now the parable is this: The seed is the word of God.

And Hosea 10:12 says:

Sow to yourselves in righteousness, reap in mercy; break up your fallow ground: for it is time to seek the Lord, till he come and rain righteousness upon you.

Since the seed is the Word and Hosea tells us to sow in righteousness, it means until you receive the word of righteousness, believe it and act on it, you will never reap any rewards.

Break up all fallow grounds, all unplowed grounds of your life. Break up the hardened habits, that sin that so easily besets you. Then God will make bright clouds and send rain upon every green grass in the field, and that includes you!

You are in a most privileged season of your life, you will not misuse His heaven -sent opportunity!

Chapter 3

THE RAIN OF
THE SPIRIT

*Be glad then, ye children of Zion, and rejoice in the
Lord your God: for he hath given you the former rain
moderately, and he will cause to come down for you
the rain, the former rain, and the latter rain in the
first month.*

*And it shall come to pass afterward, that I will pour
out my spirit upon all flesh; and your sons and your
daughters shall prophesy, your old men shall dream
dreams, your young men shall see visions.*

Joel 2:23,28

The Holy Spirit is a personality in the order of the
Godhead! He is the third Person of the Trinity, not a
feeling or an emotion (1John 5:7)!

He is in charge of the affairs of the kingdom of God on earth today, the Chief Executive of the divine programme on earth (Joel 2:28).

The Holy Spirit is the motivator, energiser and operator of every revealed plan (vision) from God. He is the revealer of the hidden treasure of the kingdom (I Cor. 2:9).

He holds the key to the inheritance of the saints, and is the most valuable asset to Christian living. He is the central figure in any breakthrough in life.

The effect of the Holy Spirit can be likened to rain. Just as rain is crucial to the sustenance of a river, the rain of the Spirit is the life wire of the river in you.

> *He that believeth on me, as the scripture hath said, out of his belly shall flow rivers of living water.*
>
> *(But this spake he of the Spirit, which they that believe on him should receive: for the Holy Ghost was not yet given; because that Jesus was not yet glorified).*
>
> John 7:38-39

The baptism of the Holy Spirit is descibed as *"rivers of living water."* But if the climate is harsh, a river reduces in volume and can ultimately dry up. So, it needs the rain to keep it full of water.

That is why you need the rain of the Spirit, to increase

the volume of "water" in your "river." Without it, you run a risk of drying up.

THE RAIN OF THE SPIRIT

Be glad then, ye children of Zion, and rejoice in the Lord your God: for he hath given you the former rain moderately, and he will cause to come down for you the rain, the former rain, and the latter rain in the first month.

Joel 2:23

Once the rain of righteousness has fallen, it paves the way for the release of the rain of the Spirit. The rain of the Spirit is the second type of rain.

God gave us the former rain moderately, but He will cause to come down for us "the rain". A combination of both the former and the latter rain, in the first month.

When the former rain fell in Acts chapter 2, Peter quoted from verses 28-32 of Joel 2. That was the former rain. Now, God declares He is going to cause to come down for us "the rain" — the former and the latter rain, in the same month!

He gave the former rain to them moderately. That means, whatever Peter, Paul and John the revelator saw were moderate. What He has prepared for us who love Him, neither Peter nor Paul, nor John saw that kind, for eyes have not seen, nor ears heard, neither has it entered into the heart of man (I Cor. 2:9). But now God is revealing it to us by His Spirit.

So, we have the former rain. The latter rain begins as prophetically declared in Isaiah 61, with the day of vengeance of our God.

> *The spirit of the Lord God is upon me; because the Lord hath anointed me to preach good tidings unto the meek; he hath sent me to bind up the broken-hearted, to proclaim liberty to the captives, and the opening of the prison to them that are bound;*
>
> *To proclaim the acceptable year of the Lord, and the day of vengeance of our God; to comfort all that mourn.*
>
> Isaiah 61:1-2

When Jesus came, He opened up the chapter for the former rain in Luke 4:18,19. The Bible says, He opened the book, and found the place where it was written:

> *The Spirit of the Lord is upon me, because he hath anointed me to preach the gospel to the poor; he hath sent me to heal the brokenhearted, to preach deliverance to the captives, and recovering of sight to the blind, to set at liberty them that are bruised,*
>
> *To preach the acceptable year of the Lord. And he closed the book...*

If you go back to Isaiah 61, from where Jesus took His

reading, you will see that He stopped at, *"To proclaim the acceptable year of the Lord."* The latter rain begins from where He closed the book. It begins with the rest of that reference in Isaiah 61:2:

... and the day of vengeance of our God...

The latter rain begins with the day of vengeance of our God, so as to comfort all that mourn! To comfort all that are afflicted and are being tormented, by bringing vengeance upon their enemies.

The latter rain is for the latter day Church. And it has started falling already.

Where the former rain stopped is where the latter rain is taking off from. A combination of the two is for this generation, culminating in diverse signs and wondes, such as have never been.

THE RAIN IS AN OUTPOURING!

And it shall come to pass afterward, that I will pour out my spirit upon all flesh; and your sons and your daughters shall prophesy, your old men shall dream dreams, your young men shall see visions.

Joel 2:28

This scripture is actually talking about the pouring out of the rain of "My Spirit". To pour means "to flow, especially downwards, in a continuous stream." It also means "to fall heavily (of rain)."

This means that the rain of the Spirit will be poured out on the people of God in the last days, releasing them to a most glorious destiny in God. It is an outpouring that will exalt the Church above all hills, and establish her above all mountains, and all nations shall flow unto her.

And because your lifting is tied to the lifting of the Church, you also need the outpouring of the rain of the Spirit to be lifted.

IT BEGINS WITH CONSECRATION

Now when they heard this, they were pricked in their heart, and said unto Peter and to the rest of the apostles, Men and brethren, what shall we do?

Then Peter said unto them, Repent, and be baptized every one of you in the name of Jesus Christ for the remission of sins, and ye shall receive the gift of the Holy Ghost.

Acts 2:37-38

With this we understand that it is impossible to encounter the outpouring of the rain of the Spirit, without righteousness being in place.

So, the rain follows consecration. It requires yieldedness. I am not talking about baptism, but the outpouring of the Spirit.

It is actually the level of your consecration to God that determines the level of unction you enjoy.

Acts 3:19 says:

Repent ye therefore, and be converted, that your sins may be blotted out, when the times of refreshing shall come from the presence of the Lord.

That is still talking about the rain of the Spirit, which will come from the presence of the Lord. When you repent and are converted and your sins are blotted out, you are then set to enjoy the times of refreshing that come by the outpouring of the Spirit.

There is coming a deluge of divine release, that will turn every destiny the right way up. But you must break up your fallow grounds. Break up that hardened habit that is out to make you a kingdom misfit. Determine to invest in righteousness; work it out, and you will experience the rain of the Spirit.

Chapter 4

THE RAIN OF THE WORD

For as the rain cometh down, and the snow from heaven, and returneth not thither, but watereth the earth, and maketh it bring forth and bud, that it may give seed to the sower, and bread to the eater:

So shall my word be that goeth forth out of my mouth: it shall not return unto me void, but it shall accomplish that which I please, and it shall prosper in the thing whereto I sent it.

Isaiah 55:10-11

The Word of God can be likened to rain that comes pouring down from heaven. It is God's major way of ending the drought in a man's life.

When the Word is received and applied, no matter how

harsh the climate, results are inevitable. Responding to the Word is the way to end the dry seasons of your life.

For instance, in the time of Isaac, there was physical famine in the land. King and subjects alike were affected. The famine was very severe and king Abimelech and all his experts saw no way out. Isaac was also in that land. He despised the famine and obeyed the Word of God — sowing inspite of the weather condition; and God blessed him. Isaac became great because he operated God's Word.

God's Word is your access to healing, deliverance, abundance, promotion, etc. Just like no amount of energy applied can force open a firmly locked door, it is only the application of the Word to a given circumstance that can produce favourable results — not the use of force. Peter said:

> *...Master, we have toiled all the night, and have taken nothing: nevertheless at thy word I will let down the net.*

Luke 5:5

God's Word is powerful. It is able to shatter the hardships of your life to pieces. When you issue commands based on the authority and integrity of the Word, you trigger the power present in it to arrest all contrary situations.

The Word, comes like rain. Remember rain comes from the heavens; similarly, a Word can come to you from heaven, making all the difference in your life. Many men who have enjoyed the lifting hand of God either in ministry, business or in whatever form, always claim that a Word came to them from God, resulting in their distinction (Isa. 55:10 -11).

When there is an outpouring of the rain of the Word and your spirit absorbs it, you "bring forth and bud" in all areas of life. Somebody shared this testimony recently:

"For 18 years, my mother suffered from hypertension. But she got hold of one of the Bishop's books, Keys to Divine Health. She read in the book that the devil is not a gentleman and immediately decided not to be taking her drugs again, but to rather claim her healing.

For over a month now, she has not taken the drugs. And when she went for a test last month, the test confirmed that her blood pressure had come down to 120/80. This has never been in the past 18 years! The test also confirmed that she does not have hypertension any more."

As she absorbed the Word in that book, it produced a harvest of divine health for her! It takes the Word therefore, to have victory over one's life's circumstances. There is nothing life demands that is not obtainable in it. That is why you need the rain of the Word to fall upon you.

CONSECRATION FIRST, THEN REVELATION

But, the rain of revelation draws from the rain of righteousness. Proverbs 1:23 says:

> *Turn you at my reproof: behold, I will pour out my spirit unto you, I will make known my words unto you.*

So, you turn at His reproof first before He pours His Spirit upon you and makes known His Words unto you. The Holy Spirit is prepared to teach you the ways of God, but until you turn away from iniquity, He will not teach you and except the Holy Spirit teaches you a thing, you cannot know it.

> *Which things also we speak, not in the words which man's wisdom teacheth, but which the Holy Ghost teacheth; comparing spiritual things with spiritual.*
>
> 1 Corinthians 2:13

Thus, without consecration, there is no unction, and without unction, there is no revelation.

So, carnality disqualifies you for the rain of insight. Verse 14 says the natural or carnal man cannot understand the things of the Spirit, because they are spiritual discerned.

So, as long as you remain carnal, you have no access

to insight into the Word. Paul said:

And I, brethren, could not speak unto you as unto spiritual, but as unto carnal, even as unto babes in Christ.

I have fed you with milk, and not with meat: for hitherto ye were not able to bear it, neither yet now are ye able.

1 Corinthians 3:1-2

THE RAIN RELEASES HEAVEN'S TREASURES

And it shall come to pass, if thou shalt hearken diligently unto the voice of the Lord thy God, to observe and to do all his commandments which I command thee this day, that the Lord thy God will set thee on high above all nations of the earth:

And all these blessings shall come on thee, and overtake thee, if thou shalt hearken unto the voice of the Lord thy God.

Blessed shalt thou be in the city, and blessed shalt thou be in the field.

Blessed shall be the fruit of thy body, and the fruit of thy ground, and the fruit of thy cattle, the increase of thy kine, and the flocks of thy sheep.

Blessed shall be thy basket and thy store.

Blessed shalt thou be when thou comest in, and

blessed shalt thou be when thou goest out.

Deuteronomy 28:1-6

All the blessings listed above are triggered off by the Word of God, they are Word released. But the journey begins with consecration. Consecration begets unction and unction results in revelation, which in turn produces manifestations of the goodness of the Lord.

The voice of God coming to you via the Word makes all the difference in all areas of your life. It is one thing to hear from a pastor, but an entirely different thing to hear from heaven. The things I am celebrating in Christ today are things I heard directly from Him.

Somebody is talking, yes; but Somebody else is explaining it to me from within, Somebody else is opening my eyes!

The things that make us are the things which the Holy Ghost teaches. However, until He is invited, He won't come. You first clear up the ground of your heart, then invite the Holy Spirit to come and teach you. You cannot be confused when He teaches you.

I remember facing terrific persecutions when I first started teaching on the subject of prosperity. But I would not be persuaded otherwise, because I knew where I got it from. I knew I heard it directly from source! No one could confuse me. Now all our detractors are preaching the same message!

This is your season to be made by the showers of heaven. You won't miss it!

IT BRINGS SATISFACTION

Wherefore do ye spend money for that which is not bread? and your labour for that which satisfieth not? hearken diligently unto me, and eat ye that which is good, and let your soul delight itself in fatness.

Isaiah 55:2

God's Word satisfies, because it is bread indeed. As you reorder your life to make hearkening to the Word the centre of your desire, you will be satisfied with goodness and fatness.

Some are hunting for blessings. But blessings come only after you have had encounters with the Word of God.

The Word of God is food for the spirit.

Thy words were found, and I did eat them; and thy word was unto me the joy and rejoicing of mine heart: for I am called by thy name, O Lord God of hosts.

Jeremiah 15:16

No food is useful to the body until it is digested. Likewise, God's Word can only have impact in your life when you digest it. Once it has been digested, its profits begin to appear.

Do you want to be satisfied with good all the days of your life? Then, the Word of God must become a part of you. It must be properly absorbed into your system for it to satisfy you.

You have read certain scriptures, but you just don't seem to feel their impact. Why? You have not yet absorbed them into your life, so they cannot satisfy you.

Take time to ponder on the things you are hearing and reading. Give more earnest attention to them (1Tim. 4:13-16).

Many hear and many read, but few take time out to think on the things they have heard and read. It is as you meditate on the Word that you draw nourishment from it and satisfaction comes.

For instance, when I found the mystery of long life and victory over death, I knew! The Word of faith can't be in you without you knowing it. I ate up the Word of faith, and I knew that there was no occultic power, no armed bandit that could cut short my life!

I have never prayed for peace in my family once! Why? I had made outstanding discoveries on marriage before I got married and not one of them has failed yet!

The Word of God satisfies! Our ministry has simply

been run on discoveries. Everything that has come forth here, came by the Word.

> *Through faith we understand that the worlds were framed by the word of God, so that things which are seen were not made of things which do appear.*
>
> Hebrews 11:3

Anything that stands between you and the Word of God is out to destroy you. There is no substitute for the Word. It is your ticket to genuine and lasting satisfaction!

Chapter 5

THE RAIN OF BLESSINGS

Then said the Lord unto Moses, Behold, I will rain
bread from heaven for you; and the people shall go
out and gather a certain rate every day, that I may
prove them, whether they will walk in my law, or no.

Exodus 16:4

There is a way to break forth into the realm, where the showers of heaven's blessings will stay with you, until you get to the borders of heaven, just as Israel was fed everyday for forty years, until they got to the border of Canaan.

Remember, God has an agenda to deck the last days' Church with honour, riches and glory such as eyes have never seen, nor ears heard. That is why God's Word says:

The silver is mine, and the gold is mine, saith the Lord of hosts.

The glory of this latter house shall be greater than of the former, saith the Lord of hosts: and in this place will I give peace, saith the Lord of hosts.

Haggai 2:8-9

So, God is going to release the rain of plenty upon the Church and make her an envy of nations. But the purpose for heaven's rain of blessing, is for the last days' Church, to take the gospel to all nations of the earth (Mk. 13:10 and Matt. 24:14).

Zechariah 1:17 buttresses this fact:

Cry yet, saying, Thus saith the Lord of hosts; my cities through prosperity shall yet be spread abroad...

This establishes the fact that heaven has budgeted all the finances necessary for the building of the latter day house.

I am persuaded that the rain of God will answer to you, flushing out lack and want and bringing you to a realm of superlative abundance.

IT IS RELEASED BY INSIGHT!

God's rain of plenty or showers of blessing is released on the basis of insight into the workings of the covenant.

*But thou shalt remember the Lord thy God: for it is
he that giveth thee power to get wealth, that he may
establish his covenant which he sware unto thy
fathers, as it is this day.*

Deuteronomy 8:18

The showers are provoked to come down for you by
covenant practices. But how can you practice what you
don't know? So, the journey to abundance begins with
knowledge.

For instance, you don't practice law because you speak
good English. No, you practice law because you have
studied law. Can you tell the judge in the court, "I can
defend myself"? And if he asks you why, you tell him,
"Because I speak good English." It is not English. If you
haven't studied law, you cannot defend yourself.

If you don't know it, you can't practise it. The same
goes for the covenant. If you don't know what it entails,
you cannot practise it.

However, once you gain access to what the covenant
entails and do it, you are set for the release of the showers
of blessings.

Deuteronomy 8:7-10 paints a very colourful picture of
the effect of the showers.

*For the Lord thy God bringeth thee into a good land,
a land of brooks of water, of fountains and depths*

that spring out of valleys and hills;

A land of wheat, and barley, and vines, and fig trees, and pomegranates; a land of oil olive, and honey;

A land wherein thou shalt eat bread without scarceness, thou shalt not lack any thing in it; a land whose stones are iron, and out of whose hills thou mayest dig brass.

When thou hast eaten and art full, then thou shalt bless the Lord thy God for the good land which he hath given thee.

Remember also that Deuteronomy 8:18 says:

But thou shalt remember the Lord thy God: for it is he that giveth thee power to get wealth...

Combining this with Deuteronomy 8:7-10, it becomes evident that God is the One who gives the power to get wealth, in order to establish His covenant.

So, we need an understanding of the covenant to enter the "good land", where you will eat bread without scarceness, and in which you will never lack anything. A land well watered by heaven's rainfall.

I have never prayed for God to give me money, or prayed for success in my ministry. No! I simply have access to the Holiest place, where the tables of the covenant are kept. When you lay hold on the tables of the covenant, you become a commander.

God shows you the things designed for you to do, and the moment you give yourself to doing them, things begin to work on their own accord.

I have never prayed for peace to reign in our home. Peace reigns in it by covenant! We have not had the first argument since we got married. There has been nothing to argue over!

Insight into the covenant triggers off showers of diverse kinds of blessings! For instance, I cannot be sick; not by the Word of divine healing, but by the covenant of divine health! When I gained entrance into those tables, I read them and found the things that must never be thought about or spoken if I want to remain healthy. So, I don't get sick, because I am operating the tables of the covenant.

It was insight into the covenant that made Job succcessful. He said:

> *As I was in the days of my youth, when the secret of God was upon my tabernacle;*
>
> *When I washed my steps with butter, and the rock poured me out rivers of oil.*
>
> Job 29: 4,6

God's rainfall answers to insight into the secrets of God! Those secrets, also known as mysteries, are located in the Word of God. And the Word is God's covenant book. That is why every blessing is anchored on what you do with what the Book contains.

> *But his delight is in the law of the Lord; and in his law doth he meditate day and night.*
>
> *And he shall be like a tree planted by the rivers of water, that bringeth forth his fruit in his season; his leaf also shall not wither; and whatsoever he doeth shall prosper.*
>
> Psalm 1:2-3

Whatever he does prospers because his delight is in the law of his God, and upon it does he meditate day and night. He is like a tree planted by the rivers of water where the showers never stop falling.

The Bible in Deuteronomy 28:1-6, 13; Isaiah 34:16 and Joshua 1:8 gives us an understanding that every blessing of life emanates from insights into the covenant. When you observe to do what is written in the Word, you make your way prosperous and you have good success.

That is why plenty answers to insight, not to struggles, nor to cries; but insight! You must begin to desire to break forth into the realm where your struggles will end.

God showed me early how to set myself for the rain of

blessings. That is why there has never been a need to gather together and pray for money in the ministry. Not even when we were six. Why? We had taken delivery of certain insights which we were practising.

You will not struggle for means any more in your life!

God has called you, to bless you. That's why the Psalmist said:

> *Blessed is the man whom thou choosest, and causest to approach unto thee, that he may dwell in thy courts: we shall be satisfied with the goodness of thy house, even of thy holy temple.*

Psalm 65:4

So, you are not called for a curse, but a blessing. Every curse of lack in your life has ended!

But it is important to know that God's rain of blessings does not respect environmental situations. So, don't imagine that things will be better for you if you were in Europe or America. No! These showers don't respect environmetal conditions. Remember, Israel was in the wilderness for forty years and God gave them manna until they got to the border of Canaan.

So, God is no respecter of persons or circumstances. What you need is insight into what releases the showers of blessings.

IT'S FOR THOSE WHO FEAR THE LORD

The secret of the Lord is with them that fear him; and he will shew them his covenant.

Psalm 25:14

The release of the showers of blessings begins with insight into the workings of the covenant. But the covenant is not for the "public". It is for those who fear the Lord!

In essence, God has given you power to get wealth so as to establish His covenant with you. But you need an understanding of what that covenant entails. This understanding is made available to you by revelation, and revelation only comes to those who fear the Lord.

Therefore, you don't know what you are missing meddling with sin. You are disconnecting yourself from insight. That is why you are still down and trodden upon.

You need consecration to encounter revelation; and revelation will culminate in a revolution when applied.

Look at Job. He was a man who feared God and eschewed evil. A perfect man. The Bible says he had seven thousand sheep, and three thousand camels, and five hundred she asses, and a very great household; so that he became the greatest man in all the east (Job 1:3).

This same man, Job, said:

> *As I was in the days of my youth, when the secret of*
> *God was upon my tabernacle.*

Job 29:4

So, the insight Job had was a function of purity. Insight answers to purity, and Job had it.

As I earlier said, the tables of the covenant are kept in the holiest of all. And it is not everyone that has access to the holiest of all.

In the old dispensation, only the high priest had access to the holiest place, and that, once a year, after sanctifying himself. Otherwise, he would be dead.

So, the tables of the covenant are not in books, but in the holiest of all. You can read the books and not gain access into the mystery behind the words. It takes consecration to take delivery of those revelations.

Otherwise, why is it that two people read the same book, one contacts revelation, the other is tired after two pages? He can't see any thing, the words are hard as brass. He has no access, no entrance.

Why? He is a man in the flesh, he is disconnected from the source. The tables of the covenant are in the holiest of all, and it takes holiness to gain access there.

Remember:

> *The secret of the Lord is with them that fear him:*
> *and he will shew them his covenant.*

Do you want the covenant? The tables are not in the books, they are not in the letters; they are in the holiest of all, where only those who fear Him have access.

It is important to note that in the kingdom we have stories and we have mysteries. Not every Christian has access to the mysteries. Many only know the stories.

David, who enjoyed the rain of plenty throughout his reign, was an upright man (Ps. 33:18-19). Because he had a testimony in the realm of abundance, he could talk about the key to it. David brought out clearly, the need for consecration before an encounter with revelations.

> *The Lord knoweth the days of the upright: and their*
> *inheritance shall be for ever.*
>
> *They shall not be ashamed in the evil time: and in*
> *the days of famine they shall be satisfied.*

Psalm 37:18-19

This scripture explains that the upright shall be satisfied; not just existing on one meal a day, but satisfied! He will call for what he wants and it will answer to him.

So, the environment is irrelevant, it is your insight which has it's foundation in righteousness that determines your welfare. That is why if you say nothing is working in your country, it is only for you. Things are working for other people. I have seen many tenants building houses and becoming landlords. So, don't say things are not working where you are. They are!

Please appreciate that all we are talking about still anchors on practical integrity, because it enhances supernatural insight, bringing you supernatural rainfall, which distinguishes you in very difficult times!

It is worth all the effort; to go into the holy of holies and take delivery of the tables of the covenant, so that our struggles can end. Get into the holy of holies for insight, so that your rain can keep falling!

I have found Him whom my heart delights in, He is the joy of the world!

Many years ago, after our second son was born and we were to name him ceremoniously, as people in this part of the world do, there was not enough money for a party. I was principal signatory to the church's account, so I could sign out some money for the occasion. But I vowed that the church's funds would not be found in my possession. The fear of God was my driving force. So,

I served a few snacks at the occasion and everyone went home.

> *Praise ye the Lord. Blessed is the man that feareth the Lord, that delighteth greatly in his commandments.*
>
> *His seed shall be mighty upon earth: the generation of the upright shall be blessed.*
>
> *Wealth and riches shall be in his house: and his righteousness endureth for ever.*
>
> Psalm 112:1-3

Do you want to see the hand of God resting on your life? Then sign in for Him. Position yourself as you walk in righteousness. Then you will find God, and when you find Him, you have found good!

Anyone who wants the showers of blessings, must first be drenched with the showers of righteousness. You must be soaked by the rain of righteousness before you encounter landmark blessings.

From Psalm 112, it is clear that for the upright, no matter how terrible the situation around him may be, no matter how terrible the economic condition of that country, God will single him out for a blessing. How else could Joseph have prospered in the prison? Although he was a slave, God lifted him.

Houses are being built in Nigeria by Nigerians living in

the country. The land is not hard. It is the fallow ground of your heart that needs to be broken up. It is that hardened habit that won't let God move in your life that must be broken!

You are in the most privileged season of your life, don't mess it up! God will not forget you, no matter how tough the situation. He will be right on the spot.

> *Unto the upright there ariseth light in the darkness: he is gracious, and full of compassion, and righteous.*
>
> *A good man sheweth favour, and lendeth: he will guide his affairs with discretion.*
>
> Psalm 112:4-5

So, it is righteousness that triggers off the showers of blessings.

SHOWERS BRING RESTORATION

When God's rain of blessings begins to fall, there is a great restoration. So that if you had lost anything in life, the release of the rain brings you a replacement of that which was lost and makes you forget that anything was ever missing!

But it begins with a returning back to the Lord with all your heart.

> *Therefore also now, saith the Lord, turn ye even to*

me with all your heart, and with fasting, and with weeping, and with mourning:

And rend your heart, and not your garments, and turn unto the Lord your God: for he is gracious and merciful, slow to anger, and of great kindness, and repenteth him of the evil.

Gather the people, sanctify the congregation...

Be glad then, ye children of Zion, and rejoice in the Lord your God: for he hath given you the former rain moderately, and he will cause to come down for you the rain, the former rain, and the latter rain in the first month.

And the floors shall be full of wheat, and the vats shall overflow with wine and oil.

Joel 2:12,13,16,23,24.

A great restoration awaits you, but it begins with a returning to the Lord with all your heart. He said, *"Sanctify the congregation."* Why? Because He is bringing a rain of restoration, a rain of blessing such as you have never known before. That's why He said:

And ye shall eat in plenty, and be satisfied, and praise the name of the Lord your God, that hath dealt wondrously with you: and my people shall never be ashamed.

Joel 2:26

I am excited because I see the showers of God coming

down upon the people, bringing restoration that lead to revolutions!

All you need now is to break up the fallow ground of your heart. It is time to seek the Lord until He comes and rain righteousness upon you. Then there will be a turn around, a revolution in your life!

Chapter 6

KEEPING YOUR HEAVENS OPEN

There are secrets you need to know, to keep your heavens perpetually open.

GOD'S DIVINE PRESENCE

And the ark of God remained with the family of Obededom in his house three months. And the Lord blessed the house of Obededom, and all that he had.

1 Chronicles 13:14

The ark of God symbolises the presence of God. Wherever the ark dwelt, there were tremendous blessings. Consider Obededom. The ark remained with his family for three months, and the Lord blessed him and his household because of this.

The presence of God was what made the difference in Obededom's family. His presence will keep the heavens over you perpetually open.

That is why the enemy constantly tries to get you out of God's presence, so that he can oppress and afflict you. But as long as you remain enveloped in God's presence, all oppositions are converted to opportunities (Ps. 114:3-7).

God's presence is the answer to an open heaven! It was His presence, I believe, that brought about a mental, psychological and intellectual awakening in Obededom. He must have been so prosperous that David saw it and envied him and finally brought the ark into the city of David (2 Sam. 6:12). God's presence always triggers off envy, because His presence is always announced by blessings.

Thou wilt show me the path of life: in thy presence is fulness of joy; at thy right hand there are pleasures for evermore.

Psalm 16:11

Please understand that the Church is in the midst of an outburst of heavenly blessings, where a little one among us will become like a thousand and a small one, a strong nation.

As you celebrate the arrival of the ark, you will step into fullness of joy. Why? In His presence is fulness of joy, and at His right hand there are pleasures (not pressures) forever more!

When God came in the midst of Israel, their captivity of four hundred years was turned overnight and gold became their luggage!

In the wilderness, because God was with them, their heavens remained open. None was feeble among their tribes. They were not permitted to thirst, for the Rock that produced water followed them. They never hungered, because God rained Manna for them daily. They were covered by a cloud in the day and the pillar of fire by night. They were guided and protected, and the wild beast had no access to them; God's presence was their sufficiency.

If God is with you, you must have proofs!

God's presence is always announced by blessings, and when He blesses, it is forever! God blessed Obededom, it was eternal. You too will encounter such blessings as would last you a life time!

In the Acts of the Apostles there was none among them that lacked. Why? God's presence was so strong.

All that retain the ark have blessings as proofs.

THE LOVE OF GOD

Jesus said unto him, Thou shalt love the Lord thy God with all thy heart, and with all thy soul, and with all thy mind.

This is the first and great commandment.

And the second is like unto it, Thou shalt love thy neighbour as thyself.

On these two commandments hang all the law and the prophets.

Matthew 22:37-40

The love of God is the platform upon which any Word of God comes to pass. It is the vital force that keeps the heavens open.

Your love for God is the pivot for the fulfilment of all prophesies recorded in scriptures. Everything rests on it. It is the intensity of your love for God that will determine the degree of accomplishment you will have.

The love of God is what keeps the showers on. There is nobody under heaven, who is genuinely addicted to God, who will not continually enjoy the showers.

Your loving Him is what keeps your heaven open and makes the best from heaven become yours.

When man fell, his love nature died, he was stripped of the nature of love. It will therefore take supernatural help for man to enter that love realm.

The love of God is made possible and easily accomplishable by the help of the Holy Spirit. He infuses the love of God into your being, and delivers you from selfishness. You need that help today.

When you succeed in walking in that kind of love, your heaven will stay open. Why? Because things work for you only to the level that you love Him.

> *And we know that all things work together for good to them that love God, to them who are the called according to his purpose.*
>
> Romans 8:28

Every struggle settles at love. When the love of God is in place, your struggles in life come to an end.

But too many are serving God, not for love but for things. That is why the Holy Spirit is given to us, to destroy self and enthrone the God Who wants to possess us. And when that God is enthroned in our hearts, our heavens remain open!

This Love Will Destroy Oppositions

David was a man after God's heart. He was in hot pursuit of God. Remember how he obtained the throne of Israel? Someone was defiling the army of God, and David said, "No! who is this uncircumsised Philistine? I would rather die than watch him continue."

Love drove him to Goliath, love brought him the victory! Love destroyed their oppositions!

Why? Because love is greater than faith (1 Cor. 13:13). So if by taking the shield of faith you quench the fiery darts of the devil, by walking in love, you quench the devil himself!

> *And we have known and believed the love that God hath to us. God is love; and he that dwelleth in love dwelleth in God, and God in him.*
>
> 1 John 4:16

That means the love of God makes you become a partaker of God. The nature of God begins to flow inside you and no opposition can handle that!

When Jesus was here, demons were screaming. Why? God was too much on His inside. In fact, He said, *"He that has seen Me has seen the Father."* And the demons screamed, "Have You come to destroy us before the time?"

That was the realm Jesus walked in then. How much more now that He is perfected? As we partake of His perfected nature, it becomes easy for us to exercise dominion on the earth.

1 John 4:17 tells us:

> *Herein is our love made perfect, that we may have boldness in the day of judgment: because as he is, so*

are we in this world.

Therefore, when our love is perfected, we represent His personality fully, leaving no room for the devil.

Do you want your heaven to stay open? Allow the love of God to reign in your heart.

The Holy Spirit sheds abroad in your heart the love of God, delivering you from the hold of self and connecting you to God.

When that is in place, every work of the flesh that stands between you and God is destroyed and the heavens over you stay open.

Giving Proves Your Love

You can keep your heavens open by demonstrating the love of God in your giving.

This is not a man-made theology but a commandment from God to guarantee that your heavens remain open.

God's love is active. It is a giving love. God Himself demonstrated this to us as He gave His only begotten Son (John 3:16).

So, it is not the love of God if it is not a giving love; not giving as a duty, but giving cheerfully. It is your love for God that makes you give cheerfully.

Moreover, because I have set my affection to the house of my God, I have of mine own proper good, of gold and silver, which I have given to the house of my God, over and above all that I have prepared for the holy house.

1 Chronicles 29:3

David's love was demonstrated in his giving life. It was not as a matter of duty, but of delight. David was delighted in God!

Moreover, because I have set my affection to the house of my God...

It was that affection that developed into devotion, and devotion developed into addiction.

Now, let me put it this way: when love is not giving, it is not love. Giving is God's authentic proof of love.

Hereby perceive we the love of God, because he laid down his life for us: and we ought to lay down our lives for the brethren.

But whoso hath this world's good, and seeth his brother have need, and shutteth up his bowels of compassion from him, how dwelleth the love of God in him?

1John 3:16-17

So, when your bowels are shut to God and to others, there is no proof that God's love is dwelling in you. You can unlock the windows of your heavens by the demonstration of love. It is not prayer or fasting, but love!

See it this way: "God so loved, He so gave. If I so love God, I will so give to God."

You may give without loving, but you cannot love without giving. People give to satisfy their religious conscience, to earn the praises of men or simply because he is the pastor of the church. Yes! You may give for whatever reason, but you cannot love and not give.

It is the intensity of your love for God that determines how wide His windows over your head will be.

Let's go back to the basics.

> *... Thou shalt love the Lord thy God with all thy heart, and with all thy soul, and with all thy mind.*
>
> Matthew 22:37

Your giving is first to God, not to your local government council or to friends. We are not philanthropists. It must be first to God.

Then, *"Thou shalt love thy neighbour as thyself."* This is the second commandment. He said, *"Whosoever does not love Me more than himself is not worthy of Me."* So, God expects us to love Him more than ourselves and we are to love our neighbours as we love ourselves. So the line is drawn.

I will never give my wife what I give to God, because we are one and I should love God more than I love myself.

I like you to understand what I am talking about. You need a heart for God to make a mark on the earth. The larger your heart for God, the greater mark you make on the earth!

The largeness of your heart is expressed in the intensity of your giving. Intensity here is not the amount but the quality of it.

If you are not a giver, prayer cannot open your heavens. Financial blessngs are not prayed for but provoked by a covenant walk — a qualitative covenant walk.

We have not prayed for food in my family, right from the onset. The opportunity has not arisen once! No, you don't pray for material blessings.It is a covenant walk that guarantees it. The heavens over you will no longer be shut!

Until you give God His place, you never have your place. Abundance answers to God addiction. When your heavens are opened, you enter into the realm of super-natural additions.

My wife's salary when she came into the ministry was about 25% of her former salary; and yet our standard of living did not drop! It is not your income, it is the covenant!

I have seen people who have been earning salaries for

over twenty years and yet have nothing to show for it. But show me a man engaged in a qualitative covenant walk and I will show you one whose life will remian like a watered garden!

That will be your experience from now on!

GO UP TO THE MOUNTAIN

Go up to the mountain, and bring wood, and build the house; and I will take pleasure in it, and I will be glorified, saith the Lord.

Ye looked for much, and, lo, it came to little; and when ye brought it home, I did blow upon it. Why? saith the Lord of hosts. Because of mine house that is waste, and ye run every man unto his own house.

Therefore the heaven over you is stayed from dew, and the earth is stayed from her fruit.

Haggai 1:8-10

To enjoy the showers and keep your heaven open, you must remain addicted to God and His affairs on the earth.

Until you mind Him and are delighted in His plan, God will not mind you or be delighted in your ways. Except you are moved by God's kingdom, your needs never move Him.

I am moved about every thing that concerns God, that is why He is moved about me.

Many have been working yet nothing seems to work. Why? Because they are not mindful of God's house, the heaven over them has been stayed from dew and the earth stayed from her fruit.

Overflowing abundance is no guess work, it is a covenant walk! God is no respecter of persons. If you want your heavens to be perpetually open, follow these principles and you will be free.

Imagine for instance, what will be the financial future of a man who wears a wristwatch worth twenty thousand dollars, but whose mother sleeps in a shanty? The same man has never paid a tithe of one thousand dollars. That is a prodigal man!

I am addicted to God, that is why He is always adding to me.

Some twenty-four years ago, I was in a place doing a vacation job and I found out that there was no church there. So, I vowed not to leave the town the same way I met it. Although I was not a pastor and had not received any call into full-time ministry, I just loved the Lord with all my heart.

A church started in that town before I left! I remember climbing palm trees and cutting down palm fronds to build the church. But God was watching. His eyes, which run to and fro in all the earth, to show Himself strong on the behalf of those whose hearts are perfect towards Him, located me. And so I can declare with all confidence that I am blessed!

It is a burning love in your soul that gets you so connected to God that nothing else comes between you and Him. Be sold out to God! It is the only way to keep your heavens open. And as long as your heavens are open, the showers will keep falling!

David said, *"I have prepared for the house of my God with all my might."* How many in the Church can say that today? But know that your showers will only fall to the extent that your heart is with God.

That was why David was so blessed. You will always have a large treasure when you maintain a large heart for God.

Friend, the Church is in her "rainy" season. You must burst forth in your giving life and increase the quality of your covenant walk, then you will see a great tomorrow.

Many years ago, we were going for an outreach and I said to the team with me, "Friends, the Lord just spoke these words to me: Bring everything in your pockets out, and don't worry about what you will eat, I will take care of it."

I don't think the others brought all they had. Some did not understand it. How do I know? Some eleven years after, those who did not fully understand are yet to find their footing in life!

But I gave all I had in my pocket, which was about one hundred and twenty naira. That's why my showers haven't stopped falling!

There is a great future for you, may God give you understanding!

I am saying this because the end-time Church will enjoy such financial and material favours that will shake the entire world! God will locate men and women into whose hands He will commit heavenly treasures that will shake the natural world. The world will be forced to respect the Church, by reason of the lifting hand of God.

Why will God do that? Because this gospel must be preached among all nations before the end comes.

> *And this gospel of the kingdom shall be preached in all the world for a witness unto all nations; and then shall the end come.*

Matthew 24:14

And how do you preach it?

> *Cry yet, saying, Thus saith the Lord of hosts; My cities through prosperity shall yet be spread abroad; and the Lord shall yet comfort Zion, and shall yet choose Jerusalem.*

Zechariah 1:17

That means that God is preparing us to become His treasures on the earth!

So, for a man to wear a wristwatch worth twenty thousand dollars, his wrist is his god! By the time somebody earns ten thousand naira in a month and he spends nine thousand naira on food, then his stomach is his god!

Anything that takes the place of God in your life is your god. Watch it! Nothing shuts the heavens over you faster than misplaced priorities. Once you open it by covenant, even the devil will be unable to do anything about it.

Please remember, you can only serve the Lord with delight when you give Him His place. Once your income comes, your tithe must go out first, then your kingdom investments, before your organised offerings.

Not to be a regular kingdom investor is an indication that you don't believe in the covenant. But it is the covenant that opens the heavens, and walking according to its dictates, keeps it perpetually open!

Your heaven will no longer be stayed from dew, nor your earth stayed from her fruit, in Jesus' name!

Chapter 7

PRAISE KEEPS THE SHOWERS ON

God has been teaching us, particularly in this book, ways to release the showers of blessings over our lives.

In this chapter, I will be sharing with you another way to keep the showers coming. It is by using the key of praise.

In praise you are appreciating God for His Person. You are worshipping Him for who He is.

It is time to go before the Lord in worship. It is time to approach His throne with a heart of gratitude. It is time to bless the Lord and adore Him. Zechariah 14:17 says:

And it shall be, that whoso will not come up of all the

families of the earth unto Jerusalem to worship the King, the Lord of hosts, even upon them shall be no rain.

Everyone is coming before the Lord, but how many are actually coming in praise or in worship? Do you want to keep the showers falling? Then begin to worship the King! Don't let anything affect your worship.

The Psalmist said:

Bless the Lord, O my soul: and all that is within me, bless his holy name.

Psalm 103:1

So, if you don't bless Him, your rain will stop. God stops blessing you when you stop blessing Him. He won't raise you if you won't praise Him.

You have to take the steps, God is constant. He is committed to honour you if you will honour Him. If you exalt Him, He will exalt you.

It is very important that we understand the place of praise in relationship to our rainfall. Praise is what keeps the heavens open, it is what keeps the rains coming.

We are in a kingdom where good things are happening all the time, praise will deliver your portion to you.

SO, GO AHEAD AND BLESS HIM!

Bless the Lord, O my soul, and forget not all his

benefits.

Psalm103:2

When you call to mind all His benefits, it helps you to bless Him. Particularly when you remember that your iniquities have all been forgiven and that you have a guarantee of a place in heaven. Your soul should readily bless Him!

Hear this, it will help you: until you are forgiven, you are not free. It is when you are forgiven that you are free from the agents of sin like lying, adultery, hatred, etc. And you know that those agents are spiritual tormentors.

But when you are forgiven, the power to go and sin no more is delivered to you. You are recovered and restored.

Jesus told the woman caught in adultery:

...Neither do I condemn thee: go, and sin no more.
John 8:11

Many people would have gone to hell except that God intervened. That is why we must celebrate Him, to keep our heavens open! A brother shared this testimony recently:

"I had a spirit *that kept tormenting me since I came into manhood. This spirit had so tormented me, that I lost so many businesses and things. It had so tormented me, that I had been praying to God, to remove the spirit from me by killing it permanently.*

Last Tuesday, as the Bishop was praying (I knew I was still battling with that spirit), I prayed to God, saying, 'This spirit is a stumbling block in my Christian life, deliver me from it and kill it.' When I got home and was still basking in the joy of the healing I received that same day, I noticed that the spirit of womanizing had been slain, I no longer feel the urge again!"

Bless the Lord for forgiving all your iniquities. The proof that you are forgiven is in the grace of liberty. God destroys your taste for sin, delivering you from returning to it again.

That is why it is the number one benefit to bless God for; not for shoes and clothes. The psalmist deliberately said, *"Forget not all His benefits"*, because forgetting His benefits gets you hardened towards God; but a remembrance of His benefits propels you into praising Him.

That was David's secret. His personal knowledge of God's benefits resulted in his life style of praise!

A deep understanding of God's benefits will produce high praises in your mouth as well.

...Who healeth all thy diseases;

Verse 3

This is another benefit to bless God for.

You don't know the value of health until you are attacked by sickness. When you are sick everything that appears to be your concern now, loses value. Sickness humbles a man. The man who is sick and cannot feed himself, cannot drink by himself, cannot use the toilet by himself, has been humbled by sickness.

For the health you enjoy, why don't you bless Him! If you don't bless Him He has every right to erase your health! Whatever you have gathered in the world by way of possessions, sickness can dissolve it in a matter of moments! We are not blessing Him for bread and butter, but for things of greater value.

Somebody has a problem with his car and then he goes ahead to accuse God. Another has lost something, so he begins to complain. When you do that, you are showing God where your heart is. You are proving to Him that your heart is not with Him, but in things.

If you bless God for your health, He gives you greater health. If you bless Him for His provisions, He will bless you with more of it. Until you bless Him, the blessings will not continue.

Please understand that you are in for an outpouring that will never end, if you will lay hold on the things God is saying now!

Who redeemeth thy life from destruction...

Verse 4

There is a redemptive package that makes you untouchable.Witches and wizards don't have access to it. That package guarantees the protective hand of God over you and all that you have.

God protects us from many things we are unaware of. He knows those who are angry that you are laughing. He knows those who are restless that you can come out of a house and call it your own. Yet you sleep and wake up unharmed, because He has hidden you in the hollow of His hand. So, it's wisdom to give thanks in everything.

The things you sorrow about make you a sorry case. You are bothered because you don't have new shoes. But you need legs to wear the shoes. If you had no legs your cries wouldn't have been for new shoes but new legs! That will not be your portion!

That is why you must be committed to blessing the Lord at all times! If you stop blessing Him, His blessings in your life will also stop! But I find that you only stop blessing God when you forget His benefits. As long as you lay His benefits to heart you never stop blessing Him.

If you bless Him for your health He will give you greater health. If you bless Him for His provisions, He will provide more for you.

As you bless Him for delivering your soul from destruction, He guarantees that you enjoy more protection.

And now, O ye priests, this commandment is for you.

If ye will not hear, and if ye will not lay it to heart, to give glory unto my name, saith the Lord of hosts, I will even send a curse upon you, and I will curse your blessings: yea, I have cursed them already, because ye do not lay it to heart.

Malachi 2:1-2

If you don't give glory to His name, He brings curses instead of blessings. God will not turn your blessings into curses!

BLESS HIM AND FLOURISH

It is a good thing to give thanks unto the Lord, and to sing praises unto thy name, O most High:

The righteous shall flourish like the palm tree: he shall grow like a cedar in Lebanon.

Psalm 92: 1,12

Your ground remains fertile and watered when you are thankful for all He has done. Blessing God moves Him to water your ground, and as the ground is watered, you begin to flourish like a palm tree.

Therfore, it is thanksgiving that moves heaven to send rain upon you. And as long as the rain keeps falling, you remain fat and flourishing, ever productive!

We are set for the greatest downpour of God's rains in the history of the Church . You will not miss your portion in it!

Behold, the Assyrian was a cedar in Lebanon with fair branches, and with a shadowing shroud, and of an high stature; and his top was among the thick boughs.

The waters made him great, the deep set him up on high with her rivers running round about his plants, and sent out her little rivers unto all the trees of the field.

Therefore his height was exalted above all the trees of the field, and his boughs were multiplied, and his branches became long because of the multitude of waters, when he shot forth.

Ezekiel 31:3-5.

Most great trees develop in rain forests. It is the abundance of rain in the rain forest that nourishes the giant trees to full stature. So also, when you live a praiseful, thankful life, God sends you abundance of rain, which in turn shoots you up as the Cedar of Lebanon.

"The waters made him great." The waters will make you great too! I see every dry area in your life becoming like a well watered garden. You will not suffer frustration anymore!

I remember a young man who testified sometime ago. Things were not working for him, but he heard me say, "If what you are selling is not moving, place it on the ground and dance around it." And he did.

The following day, he put the items on his shoulders and began to hawk them. Suddenly, a car pulled up beside him and the driver of the car said, "Where did you get that merchandise from?" To which he replied, "I am a salesman." The driver of the car then asked him to join him in the car and drove him somewhere. Arriving at their destination, the brother was offered the post of a manager in the same factory that produced the goods he was hawking a few minutes ago!

That is how it has been with me too. I don't have one thing to complain about. I am simply dancing around my life, and it has remained watered.

The mystery behind the cedar of Lebanon hinges on this: you praise God and the rain comes. And as the rain comes, you are raised! But you can be raised higher than your present position, if you engage in high praises. So, go for it!

Let the high praises of God be in their mouth, and a two-edged sword in their hand.

Psalm149:6

There are no general blessings. You must find a place for yourself in this great outpouring of grace! God does not need anything from you. Your blessing Him is a response to His benefits which He first endowed upon you.

Let everything within you praise the Lord, then He will raise you. Complaining compounds your problems; choose rather a life of genuine praises!

Chapter 8

"GOD IS IN YOUR MIDST!"

Then shall we know, if we follow on to know the Lord: his going forth is prepared as the morning; and he shall come unto us as the rain, as the latter and former rain unto the earth.

Hosea 6:3

Everytime God comes in the midst of a people, there is such an outpouring of blessings to authenticate His presence (Ps. 16:11). He comes prepared to release upon His people beauty, honour, promotions and diverse blessings.

Let me go back a bit in history. The highest form of civilisation took place around the mediterranean, evidenced by the Egyptian Pyramids and other epitomes of ancient civilisation. That region is believed to be the site where the Garden of Eden was located, before God folded up His affairs on the earth. So, the residue of the life of God was what made for the unique civilisation in that area.

But then, the whole world became covered with darkness up until the 1400's. There was no first or third world, every nation was struggling on the "floor"!

Then Martin Luther came and sparked off the light that led to the great reformation. That light penetrated the darkness of the dark ages, and out of it grew what is known as the technological revolution. Again, it was God's presence brought about by Luther that inaugurated the heavyweight inventions in the West.

Every time the light of the Gospel grew dim, life would become stagnant again.

Later, the light penetrated America and there was an outburst of pentecostalism and shortly after, the mighty healing revivals. The aftermath of that revival is the computer technology. It was God's presence that brought about the jump in inventions.

The high level of intelligence man is currently displaying is as a result of the life of God, released by those mighty awakenings. Every awakening is accompanied with showers of blessings. Why? *"... His going forth is prepared as the morning; and he shall come into us as the rain..."*

Joel 2:23-24 points out what happens when the rain comes:

> **Be glad then, ye children of Zion, and rejoice in the Lord your God: for he hath given you the former rain moderately, and he will cause to come down for you the rain, the former rain, and the latter rain in the first month.**
>
> **And the floors shall be full of wheat, and the vats shall overflow with wine and oil.**

That's why every awakening is accompanied by downpours of blessings.

We are in one of such times again! God has sparked off a fire of revival in the Church. It has become a worldwide awakening, which will culminate in the return of the Lord Jesus Christ.

You must position yourself appropriately in God, to be at the forefront of what He is doing in our days.

NOW, YOU ARE IGNITED

3 John 2 says:

> **Beloved, I wish above all things that thou mayest prosper and be in health, even as thy soul prospereth.**

In a revival, the spirit of a man comes alive. When his spirit comes alive, it ignites his soul and affects his body, causing his entire system to come alive.

The prosperity of the soul must preceed the prosperity of the body, resulting in mental, psychological and intellectual awakening, bringing about creativity. Once there is an awakening, the life of God begins to flow everywhere, upgrading the mentality of mankind.

You are in the most exciting season of your life. You will not die in drought when there is provision for you to be watered by heaven. When Jesus came, He said, *"My Father is with Me."* And men marvelled at His wisdom. He was impeccable. His mentality was higher than His country men. He did not go to school, but He was teaching everybody who went to school.

If every awakening brings about liftings as a result of a touch on our mental faculties, let us now expect a worldwide impact in the business, scientific and technological world.

Please understand that we are on the verge of an outbreak of heavenly blessings upon the Church. A little one among us shall indeed become a thousand, and a small one a strong nation!

God has come in our midst, and His presence confers automatic blessings.

Thou wilt show me the path of life: in thy presence is fulness of joy; at thy right hand there are pleasures for evermore.

Psalm 16:11

So, in this revival we must ensure we do what guarantees His presence, because pleasures cannot come except through Him.

God's presence is upon the earth!

We are children born in due season. There will be no dryness around you. Now expect His showers!

Chapter 9

NOW, IT'S RAINING!

Look at these testimonies:

MY MONTH OF RAINFALL

"The month of April was really my month of rainfall! I have never experienced such in my life. Due to obedience to what you've been teaching us, I'm enjoying the fullness of God.

In March, I had triple promotions! On April 2nd I was blessed with 15,000 naira. On April 11th, I was again blessed with 15,000 naira. On April 12th, I bought a plot of land in my village. On April 15th I was blessed with 1,500 naira. On 25th I was blessed with 10,000 naira!

I don't play with my tithe, because I can't tie down my

destiny. Instead of paying the normal amount, I always increased it.

However, what surprised me most was that even in my sleep I was praising God! So when I woke up this morning, before going to the office, I danced very well and at about 3 p.m. today, someone blessed me with 8,000 naira! God is wonderful! There has been no struggle for anything at all this year. Things come with ease for me.

There was another piece of land which somebody wanted me to buy at 35,000 naira. He said I could take it, even if I don't have the money to pay for it now. But I told him we don't buy things on credit in my church.When he insisted and said I should pay any amount that I could afford, I gave him 12,000 naira cash, promising to pay the balance on Friday 2nd of May. This is the Lord's doing!

I am also into rental services by the help of God, without looking up to any man! So, I give Him the praise. I didn't dream of all these achievements at this age, but by words that I keep hearing on this mountain, my spirit is highly lifted."

— **Ogunbitan, O.**

BUSINESS TURNAROUND!

"I started worshipping here last September. The problem I had with my work was what brought me here.

I'm a block maker. But since 1993, the business slumped. All I did to revamp it was to no avail.

A friend invited me here, telling me that if I joined Winners' Chapel, I would be a winner. I decided to be a Winner and I came here. But all the while, I was still playing with sin. I came here, and the Bishop said whoever comes here and continues in sin would remain the same. I caught it and resolved from that day I would have nothing to do with sin again.

I forgot all about sin and changed to the law in the Bible. I read Deuteronomy 28 and started studying it. I attended last month's anointing service, the one we had thrice. After the service, I went to my work place and anointed it.

That very day, a friend came to me and said, 'Mr Laiwola, I brought this woman to you, for you to make blocks for her.' I asked how many she wanted and she said she needed about 3,000! The first miracle brought in 56,000 naira! Before I finished that one, another one came in and so it has been ever since. Now, I produce blocks everyday!"

— **Olaiwola, G. A.**

TOTAL TRANSFORMATION!

"Before I became born again on July 6th, 1996, I'd been smoking cigarettes for 10 years. I was also into woman-

izing. But when I look back at what God has done in my life, the way He has turned my life around, I can't but feel that He has been very good to me.

Not only that, God has used me to touch other people's lives. I get up in buses and begin to share the Gospel of Jesus with them.

Yesterday night, after the message, a man came down and said, 'Brother, every thing you said was directed at me.' I said, 'Well I don't know you before. I wasn't the one talking to you, it was God.' He then said I should keep praying for him and gave me some money to sow as seed for him in my church."

— Akinfemi, B.

NO BORROWING, NO BEGGING!

"On Sunday, the Bishop taught us about getting striking insights from the Word of God, saying that it is this striking insights that gives birth to signs.

Before, when I have need of anything, I go asking people for it. But after this teaching, the Spirit ministered to me, that the Bishop was referring to me, that it was because Deuteronomy 28:12 was not striking in me yet, that was why I kept going to people for help. The Spirit then ordered me back to the Word, to read it and stand upon it.

I obeyed. I read the Word and meditated upon it for

more than one hour. Then something rose in my spirit, that I should not borrow and beg any more.

I then picked up my biro and listed out all I needed, including a ceiling fan, reading table, a new Bible and money for my school. After the service that Sunday, I had only five naira in my pocket; but I didn't feel any how. Rather, I gave thanks to God and went for evangelism.

In the evangelism team, a man was looking for me. He said he wanted me to fill a form for him. I filled it and as I was about to leave, he called me back saying, 'I have something for you.' He then handed me an envelope and on opening it, it was 1,000 naira cash in it! Also, I was blessed with a new Bible.

I had earlier discussed with someone, that I needed a reading table. That same day, the man called me and said, 'This is your chair and table. You can pay me whenever you have the money.' Today again, as I went out to share the testimony with the pastors, a man came to me saying, 'I've been looking for you.' He said somebody gave him something for me. And it was 1,200 naira cash! And I had only five naira in my pocket."

— **Olaiwola, F.**

BACK PAIN HEALED!

"I had some pains in my back for over two months. As

a believer, I took the anointing oil and all I knew to do, but the pains continued. I told a friend of mine of the pain and he prescribed a drug for me. I took the medicine, but rather than being healed, the pains grew worse.

I then went to the Lord and said, 'Father, forgive me. I know that Your Word says if any man is sick, let him call upon the elders and the prayer of the elders and their laying on of hands shall heal him.' I asked God for the forgiveness of my sins.

And yesterday, when the Bishop made the altar call, I came out to give my life to Christ again, because I knew I had entered into sin, which resulted in the pains.

As the Bishop went on to make some prophetic declarations, I asked a sister for some anointing oil and anointed my head. When he said we should place our hands on our heads, I obeyed and he went on to curse every sickness in our bodies. I also placed my left hand upon my back and said, 'Father, today marks the end of pains in my life.' And immediately I had a sound in my back, as if someone was stretching my back! And now, I can do all things; I can stretch my back without any pains!"

— **Bro. Roberts**

ABOUT THE *Author*

Dr. David Oyedepo is the President and Founder of Living Faith Church Worldwide a.k.a. Winners' Chapel International, with a network of churches across all cities, towns and most villages of Nigeria and over 60 other nations that spread across five major continents of the world. His faith-based teachings have literally transformed millions of lives.

To date, he has published over 60 highly impactful titles covering a range of issues, with over seven million copies in circulation.

He is the Senior Pastor of the 50,000 - seat church sanctuary - Faith Tabernacle, Canaan Land, Ota, a suburb of Lagos, Nigeria reputed to be the largest church auditorium in the world, where presently four services run every Sunday morning.

As an educationist, his mission is currently leading a revolution in education in Nigeria, with the establishment of educational institutions at all levels - primary, secondary and tertiary including the renowned Covenant University and the newly established Landmark University, where he serves as Chancellor. His educational movement is fast spreading to other African nations.

He is married to Faith and they are blessed with sons and daughters.

Books By Dr. David Oyedepo

- The Unlimited Power Of Faith
- In Pursuit Of Vision
- Pillars Of Destiny
- Signs & Wonders Today
- Exploits In Ministry
- Winning The War Against Poverty
- Walking In Dominion
- Possessing Your Possession
- The Wisdom That Works
- Exploits Of Faith
- Anointing For Exploits
- Understanding The Power Of Praise
- Walking In Newness Of Life
- Maximise Destiny
- Commanding The Supernatural
- Winning Invisible Battles
- Success Systems
- Understanding Financial Prosperity
- Success Strategies
- Understanding Your Covenant Right
- Miracle Meal
- Exploring the Riches of Redemption
- Anointing For Breakthrough
- Excellency Of Wisdom
- Breaking Financial Hardship
- The Release Of Power
- Walking In The Miraculous
- Satan Get Lost!

- The Winning Wisdom
- Walking In Wisdom
- The Healing Balm
- Manifestations Of The Spirit
- Breaking The Curses Of Life
- Overcoming Forces Of Wickedness
- You Shall Not Be Barren!
- Exploring The Secrets Of Success
- Winning Prayer
- Understanding The Anointing
- Fulfilling Your Days
- Towards Mental Exploits
- Understanding Vision
- Understanding Divine Direction
- The Force Of Freedom
- Born To Win
- The Shower Of Blessing
- Riding On Prophetic Wings
- All You Need To Have All Your needs Met
- Operating In The Supernatural
- Ruling Your World
- The Blood Triumph
- Keys To Divine Health
- Winning Faith
- Conquering Controlling Powers
- Put Your Angels To Work
- Covenant Wealth
- Keys To Answered Prayer
- Miracle Seed
- The Hidden Covenant Of Blessing

INSIDE VIEW OF
Faith Tabernacle

Dr. David Oyedepo is the founding president of the Living Faith Church Worldwide Inc. And senior pastor of the Faith Tabernacle, a 50,000 capacity sanctuary located in Canaan Land, Ota, a suburb of Lagos Nigeria.

The construction of this gigantic architectural masterpiece was completed within twelve months and dedicated on September 18, 1999. Built totally debt free and without any foreign inputs! To God alone be all the glory.

Today, Faith Tabernacle stands as the home of signs and wonders for men and women all over the world who keep coming in droves to worship the King of kings and Lord of lords, Jesus Christ the Son of the Living God.

OUTSIDE VIEW OF FAITH TABERNACLE

CHURCH MASS TRANSIT— Over 250 buses commuting the worshippers to Church from all nook and crannies of Lagos & environs

Visit our website for more information: www.davidoyedepoministries.org

Aerial View Of Covenant University

College of Business & Social Sciences

Covenant University

Dr. David Oyedepo is the visioner and Chancellor of Covenant University founded 21st October 2002. Today, Covenant University has student population of over 6,000, all fully boarded on campus; in a state of the art halls of residence. All degree programmes offered at Covenant University are fully accredited by the appropriate accrediting body. As at date, CU offers 42 degree programmes in 3 different faculties:

COLLEGE OF SCIENCE AND TECHNOLOGY:
Computer Science, Management Information System, Architecture, Building Technology, Estate Management, Industrial Mathematics, Industrial Chemistry, Industrial Physics, Biochemistry, Biology, Microbiology, Computer Engineering, Information and Communication Technology, Electrical and Electronic Engineering, Civil Engineering, Mechanical Engineering, Chemical Engineering, Petroleum Engineering.

COLLEGE OF HUMAN DEVELOPMENT:
Philosophy, Psychology, Counseling, English Language, Mass Communication, Public Relations and Advertising, Sociology and French.

COLLEGE OF BUSINESS AND SOCIAL SCIENCES:
Accounting, Taxation and Public Sector Accounting, Banking and Finance, Business Administration, Marketing, Industrial Relations and Human Resource Management, Economics, Demography and Social Statistics, International Relations, Political Science, Public Administration, Policy and Strategic Studies.

Visit our website for more information: **www.covenantuniversity.com**

More Facilities@ Covenant University

College of Science & Technology

University Library (Centre For Learning Resources)

4,000 Seat Students Chapel

More Facilities@ Covenant University

Post Graduate Building

Senior Staff Residential Quarters

Covenant University 100 Room Ultra Modern Guest House

Students Hall Of Residence

Landmark University

Senate Building

L andmark University is a product of the education mandate given to Dr. David Oyedepo. Dedicated on the 21st of March 2011, it is the second university to be established by his ministry.

The vision of the university is to raise leaders with particular emphasis of promoting agricultural enterprise among others with a learning focus that makes a graduate bread winners, job creators and solution providers

The teaching, research and community service of the university are weaved around the intellectual and natural resource endowment of her immediate community.

Landmark University Offer the following courses:

COLLEGE OF AGRICULTURAL SCIENCES:
General Agriculture, Animal Science, Plant Science, Agricultural Extension & Rural Development, Agricultural Economics.

COLLEGE OF SCIENCE & ENGINEERING:
Industrial Chemistry, Industrial Mathematics, Industrial Physics, Computer Science, Biology, Biochemistry, Microbiology, Electrical And Information Engineering, Mechanical Engineering, Chemical Engineering, Civil Engineering, Agricultural Engineering.

COLLEGE OF BUSINESS & SOCIAL SCIENCES:
Accounting, Banking And Finance, Business Administration, Economics, Sociology, Political Science, International Relations.

Visit our website for more information: **www.landmarkuniversity.edu.ng**